Southern
Messenger
Poets

Dave Smith, Editor

THE HA-HA

poems

DAVID KIRBY

Louisiana State University Press

Baton Rouge   2003

Cloth
12   11   10   09   08   07   06   05   04   03
5   4   3   2   1
Paper
12   11   10   09   08   07   06   05   04   03
5   4   3   2   1

DESIGNER: Barbara Neely Bourgoyne
TYPEFACE: Sabon
PRINTER AND BINDER: Thomson-Shore, Inc.

Library of Congress Cataloging-in-Publication Data:

Kirby, David, 1944–
   The ha-ha : poems / David Kirby.
       p. cm.
   ISBN 0-8071-2893-7 (cloth : alk. paper) — ISBN 0-8071-2894-5 (pbk. : alk. paper)
   I. Title.
   PS3561.I66H23 2003
   811'.54—dc21   2003009437

The paper in this book meets the guidelines for permanence and durability of the Committee on Production Guidelines for Book Longevity of the Council on Library Resources. ∞

 This publication is supported in part by a grant from the National Endowment for the Arts.

Versions of these poems appeared in the following magazines: *Agni*: "The Little Sisters of the Sacred Heart"; *Cimarron Review*: "France/Francine's Begonias"; *Five Points*: "Americans in Italy," "Public Idiot," "The Search for Baby Combover," "The Werewolf"; *Kenyon Review*: "Borges at the Northside Rotary"; *Mid-American Review*: "A Man Like You but Older"; *Paris Review*: "The Elephant of the Sea"; *Ploughshares*: "The Ha-Ha, Part II: I Cry My Heart, Antonio"; *Salt Hill*: "Calling Robert Bly"; *Smartish Pace*: "Lame As a Robin"; *Southern Review*: "The Fugawi"; *TriQuarterly*: "Looking for Percy Sledge"; *Western Humanities Review*: "On My Mother's Blindness."

Contents

For the architects

THE HA-HA

The Ha-Ha, Part I: The Tao of Bo Diddley

We're staying with Barbara's parents on Oahu,
          and the first night
      we're there, I notice an angry-looking man is staring at me

out of the neighbor's upstairs window
          and mumbling something,
      but the second night I realize it's that poster of Bo Diddley

from the famous Port Arthur concert, and there's a phone wire
          in front of his face
      that bobs up and down when the trade winds blow,

which they do constantly, making it seem as though
          Mr. Diddley is saying something to me,
      even though I have no idea what it is.

The next day, two Danish girls disappear
          while backpacking,
      and at first everyone says they'll turn up soon, no problem,

but by the end of the week, most people figure those two girls
          are in *some*body's stewpot!
      Their parents arrive and make teary appearances on TV,

and everyone's completely hysterical: if this could happen to these girls,
          it could happen to the person
      you love most in this world. It could happen to you.

Barbara's father takes me for breakfast to the Officers' Club
          at Hickam Air Force Base
      every morning and tells me stories about World War II,

like the time he opens a hatch one day and sees a head
          rolling across the deck
      of the USS *White Plains:* it belongs to a kamikaze pilot

whose plane has been shot to pieces just seconds before
          and whose face has been
      captured in a photo taken by another sailor just seconds before that,

and in the photo, the pilot's eyes are shut tightly, because
                    as his plane rose into the sky,
          surely the pilot thought, "I love the Emperor!" and then,

when he saw his target, "I must hit the ship's fuel tanks,
                    so the destruction will be truly terrible!"
          but as the photo's being snapped, he thinks what you or I would

if we were kamikaze pilots in the last seconds of life: "Dunnngg!"
                    Sometimes I think I've read
          just about everything written on the subject of death,

but I still don't get it: when my own father died eight years ago,
                    it was like throwing a switch;
          he was alive, and then he was dead, just like that.

A week after we return to the mainland, the Danish girls
                    are found on a ledge,
          living on rainwater and breath mints, and everyone's overjoyed,

not the least all local males between 18 and 45
                    with police records!
          Later, they'll laugh about this—the Danes, that is,

and their big Danish brains will save them from madness,
                    for aren't the stories
          that make us happiest the ones that sit astride our minds

like toads, like huge leaky tumors, and doesn't my own brother
                    not just like but *love* to think
          of how baffled our parents were when he screamed each time

the train went by and how finally one night they overheard
                    the babysitter, whose name
          was Teen, saying to Albert as he squirmed in his high chair

that if he didn't eat his vegetables, the train was going to
                    jump off the track
          and come over and "squash the blood out of him"?

Death scares the bejeezus out of you when you're a kid. A pet dies,
or a grandparent: "I'm next!" you shout.
You're a kid, though, so you're laughing! Always laughing!

When I think of Oahu now, I don't see the blue waters
or the wrinkled mountains with clouds
behind which the gods might be smoking a little *pakalolo;*

instead I see Bo Diddley hanging on that boxy-looking guitar,
his face a mask of stoicism as he says,
"Genius is the activity which repairs the decays of things,"

which Emerson said before him, but no matter: to quote a genius
is a kind of genius itself,
is a stay against confusion, like a ha-ha, like a ditch with a wall

at the bottom that lets cows and sheep appear as part
of the landscape but keeps them
from screaming and shitting under your window.

Or maybe Mr. Diddley's saying "I don't believe in God,
but I'm afraid of Him,"
a line many attribute to the Kevin Spacey character

in *The Usual Suspects* but which is actually from a short story
by Gabriel García Márquez
and probably somebody else before him.

And the kamikaze pilot? Surely he is
in heaven now, as young as he ever was,
and at the Emperor's right hand.

"On the other hand, Surveyors are runnin' about numerous as Bed-bugs, and twice as cheap, with work enough for all certainly in Durham at present, Enclosures all over the County, and North Yorkshire,—eeh! Fences, Hedges, Ditches ordinary and Ha-Ha Style, all to be laid out . . . I could have stay'd home and had m'self a fine Living . . . ?"

"They did mention a Background in Land-Surveying," Mason in some Surprize, "but, but that's it? Hedges? Ha-Has?"

"Well, actually the Durham Ha-Ha boom subsided a bit after Lord Lambton fell into his, curs'd it, had it fill'd in with coal-spoil."

—THOMAS PYNCHON, *Mason & Dixon*

Tragedy is underdeveloped comedy.

—PATRICK KAVANAGH

The Fugawi

I'm walking up Park toward Grand Central
    when the second prostitute in as many blocks says,
"Hey, Dave! Wanna date?"
        and I, fresh from my first MLA session,
want to say, "You—you know me?

Did—did you listen to my paper on foreshortening
    in Henry James's novels?"
but then I realize I've left my name tag on,
        and suddenly my lovely navy-blue blazer
morphs into a pair of bib overalls,

and a straw hat appears on my head
    as a front tooth goes mysteriously missing . . .
It's me, folks, *Hickus americanus,*
        just off the boat he poled up the East River
and left at the dock on the end of Fulton Street,

crying, "Hootie-hoot!" as he makes his way
    over the whitebait, the sea bass,
the pike and walleye, "Hootie-hoot, y'all!
        It's me! It's Dave!
Y'all know me? I love yooouu! Hootie-hoot!"

Back on Park, the people I am with
    are laughing at me—hard.
They are holding their stomachs and weeping
        and going, "Bleh-heh-heh-heh!"
and I want to say to them,

Laugh while you can, my overeducated amigos—
    nobody even snickered when I said,
"Insurance investigator"as Mrs. Carruth went around
        our eighth-grade classroom asking everybody
what they wanted to be when they grew up,

because in those days, there were these matchbooks
    advertising the correspondence course you'd take

to learn how to shadow people, lift prints, detect lies,
             and the ad promised good pay, steady work, prestige,
and there was even a picture of a guy who looked like our dads—

better than our dads, even, more like Fred MacMurray
             in *Double Indemnity* with the fedora and the snappy patter
and the dame who'd eventually betray him.
             My dad was an English professor, and I, not wanting
to be him, became him. The suit I'm wearing on Park

cost 40 bucks when I was a senior in college,
             and people still compliment me on being able to wear it
even now, decades later, but the truth is I was pretty chunky
             back then, I lived on cheeseburgers and Budweiser,
and it's only now, after years of job stress

and meal-skipping that I'm able to get back into
             that suit again—not thanks to sandwiches and beer
this time but to *foie gras* and expensive Bordeaux.
             Same suit, different guy—or not? Stanley Kubrick said,
"Gentiles don't know how to worry":

could be I am congenitally unable
             to figure these things out, am a member
of the tribe that was so stupid that it wandered
             the hills and valleys crying, Where the Fugawi?
And do we know, and do we want to know,

and if we do, are we not like the doting husband
             who realizes to his horror that the alabaster body
of his beloved is a "dormitory from Hell"
             harboring six alternate personalities, all of whom
have distinct identities, voices, even appearances

and who is told by her therapist yeah, sure,
             I can make her core personality step out of that inferno,
but what you get in the end might not be
             the darling you married, might be the kleptomaniac,
the arsonist, the crazy nun, the nympho?

When the Roman mob chased Cinna the poet,
             crying, "Kill him, he's a traitor!"

he answered, "I'm not Cinna the politician,
         I'm Cinna the poet!" and the mob cried,
"Kill him for his bad verses!"

and as I think of that, I can feel my jeans and t-shirt loosen
         and pull away and become a toga, then a pair of overalls,
then a gabardine sports coat as I say, "I'm Cinna the poet,"
         then "Hootie-hoot!" then "Okay, lady,
where were you when the officers found his corpse?"

The Werewolf

I first started giving poetry readings
        about the time I rediscovered Whitman—
I'd been writing like Dickinson and Gerard Manley Hopkins,
        and people would say, "Hmm, nice!"
or "Now that's some interesting language there!"

But then I started reading Father Walt,
        he of the tousled locks and the vast, unkempt beard,
progenitor of all those bastards (or so he said
        to woo the homophobes of his day),
and, after that, *his* fathers, the Hebrew poets

of the Old Testament with their towering accretions
        of rhetoric that just built and built and built,
and my own poems started getting longer and—
        well, damn it, *better,* I thought, only if there's nobody there
to hear them, then what's the point?

So I began to write letters to the newspaper denouncing myself:
        the first time I did it, I was Rollie Butkus,
the Pensacola shop teacher who'd been
        driving back from the shop teachers' convention
in Tampa and who'd got sick from something

he ate at the Roy Rogers on I-75 and had decided
        to spend the night in Tallahassee and had started
feeling better but had then wandered into the damned reading
        by mistake, which just made him feel worse again,
but at least now he was back in Pensacola

and wasn't spending every day sitting on the pot
        all the time, though the thing he still can't get over
is that for the life of him he couldn't find
        a single American value in this Kirby's poetry,
and this bastard is a professor, damn it!

And the next time I was Muffie Winkelberry, the sorority girl
        who didn't want to go to the reading but went anyway

with one of her sisters who didn't want to go either
        but had to for the extra credit,
and she, Muffie (not Jingle, this other girl

who needed the extra credit because even though
            she'd turned in all her assignments on time,
she'd missed too many classes on account of
        having been up all night painting banners
and leading singalongs and doing all the stuff

that somebody's got to do if she's assistant rush chairman,
            which is a big job for somebody who was just a pledge herself
a semester ago), had always heard that poetry was pretty,
        but there was nothing pretty about this so-called poet's poetry
as far as she, Muffie, was concerned!

And some people would tell me
            they couldn't believe that stupid idiot who wrote
that stupid letter to the stupid newspaper,
        and others would stop me in the hall and say,
"David, you wrote that letter, didn't you?"

I didn't care whether they knew or not;
            in fact, it was better if they thought I did, really,
because then either they loved me more
        for my inventiveness and sense of humor
or hated me more for calling more attention to myself,

either of which was fine by me,
            since I pretty much loved and hated myself
in equal measure, much as the werewolf does,
        this repulsive creature that everybody loathes
but that's also savage, well-muscled, omnipotent,

just as each of us thinks of himself
            as this wild-haired beast that's sure
it deserves the contumely and spittle of passersby,
        even as we revel in the secret knowledge
that we can rip the bastards' throats out

with a single swipe of our filthy paw.
            Yes, folks, poetry is powerful shit, all right:

it can cure ya or kill ya.
    And the poet himself:
he's quite a fellow, isn't he? Or a gal, if it's a her.

I believe it was Marie-Jean Hérault de Séchelles
        who said, "Tell many people that your reputation
is great; they will repeat it, and these repetitions
        will make your reputation." Of course no one knows
who Marie-Jean Hérault de Séchelles is today.

It could be he chose not to heed his own counsel.
        Bad mistake, that: if you've got a good idea, best put it into
practice so people can see you talk the talk *and* walk the walk.
        Poor Marie-Jean: he sacrificed himself,
the way the truly great ones do.

The werewolf also is a kind of Christ figure: he drools for our sins.
        And what are those? Let's see, excessive self-love and . . .
oh, come on, reader, I love myself, sure,
        but don't you know I love you, too—
don't you know I'm Mr. Walt's boy, li'l Dave?

Someone Naked and Adorable

When I see the sign that says "Nude Beach,"
       I scuttle right over, though when I get there,
all I see is three guys who look like me,
       two in baggy Kmart-type bathing suits
and one in a "banana hammock" of the type favored
       by speed racers and the lesser European nobility,

and as they wait for the naked people to appear,
       all three scowl at the sand, the water,
the very heavens themselves, the clouds
       as raw as the marble from which Bernini
carved the Apollo and Daphne whose bodies rang like bells
       when the restorers touched them,

like the bells of Santa Croce that summer
       that woke me and Barbara every morning
in Florence, which we called, not "Florence,"
       but "Guangdong Province," because
Hong Kong was in the news a lot in those days,
       and Hong Kong is near Guangdong Province,

and the bells would go guang! dong! as though
       a drunken priest were swinging from the bellrope.
Now surely that is "the music of the spheres"
       (Sir Thomas Browne) as opposed to
"the still, sad music of humanity" (Wordsworth),
       which is just some guy playing a violin in the corner.

Or four guys: a string quartet, and not a good one, either,
       one that meant well but hadn't practiced
very much, or maybe one that hadn't even
       meant well, that just wanted to get paid,
maybe meet a scullery maid or two,
       perhaps a nymphomaniacal marchioness . . .

What the hell do people want, anyway?
       Why does Barbara adore the cameo I gave her
that depicts Leda and the swan, an episode
       in interspecies relationships that just gives me
the creeps? There must be something there
       about being, not dominated, but overcome—

about allowing oneself to be mastered
        by a force greater than oneself
or just another person who has taken on
        temporary godlike powers,
for life has a sting in its tail, like a chimera,
        and you can no more draw that sting yourself

than you can tickle yourself,
        whereas another person can do both.
Why, in the "cabinet of secrets"
        of the Archeological Museum in Naples,
I saw a bell in the shape of a gladiator at war
        not with another warrior but with his own *Schwanz*!

It had rolled up on its back,
        if a penis can be said to have a back,
and was clawing and snapping at its master
        with the nails and teeth of a lion!
And in turn he, the gladiator, was slashing back
        with a broadsword in one hand and some kind

of lion-slapper or *Schwanz*-slapper in the other!
        Slap, slap, slice, slap! That would sting,
wouldn't it? And it's a bell, remember,
        so the whole was meant to be struck
and struck hard, be it by angry bachelor
        or vengeful wife! Dong! And given the choice

of which part of the bell to strike,
        who wouldn't strike the pecker-penis,
the ravening lion of unrequited desire?
        As if to say, *you*'re the one who's causing
all the problems, *you*'re the one body part
        who's making trouble for all the others!

No, no, we want something else altogether,
        for, as wise old Mr. Emerson says in
A Room with a View, Love is not the body
        but is of the body, the one we are waiting for
there on the beach, rooted in the sand like shore birds,
        our every atom tingling with desire.

Americans in Italy

As I wait in line to get into Vasari's Corridor,
which stretches from the Palazzo Vecchio to the Pitti Palace
        and along which Cosimo de' Medici could walk without
the bodyguard he employed to keep the thugs of the Albizi
        or the Pazzi families from sticking their knives in him,
I am passed by dozens of my countrymen and -women,
        most of whom are dressed as though they're here
not to look at the Botticellis and the Ghirlandaios
        but to play city-league softball or mow the lawn.

The three things Americans visiting Italy worry about most
are (1) being cheated, (2) being made to eat something
        they don't like, and (3) being cheated in the course
of being made to eat something they don't like.
        To these people, I say: Americans, do not worry.
Italians will not cheat you. Dishonesty requires calculation,
        and Italians are no fonder of calculation than we are.
As for the food, remember that you are in a restaurant,
        for Christ's sake, and therefore it is highly unlikely

that your handsome, attentive waiter will bring you
a bunch of boiled fish heads, much less a bowl of hairspray soup
        or a slice of tobacco pie topped with booger ice cream.
Indeed, you have already been both cheated and made to eat
        bad food in your so-called Italian restaurant in Dearborn
or Terre Haute where the specialty is limp manicotti
        stuffed with cat food and welded to an oversized ashtray
with industrial-strength tomato sauce; therefore be not
        like the scholar in *The Charterhouse of Parma*

who never pays for the smallest trifle without looking up
its price in Mrs. Starke's *Travels,* where it states how much
        an Englishman should pay for a turkey, an apple,
a glass of milk, and so on, but eat, drink, and spend freely,
        for tomorrow you will again be in Grand Rapids or Fort Wayne.
As Cosimo strolled his corridor, he could glance out from time to time
        to see if three or four of the abovementioned Pazzi or Albizi
were gathering to discuss something that almost certainly
        would not have been a surprise birthday party for him.

Also, he could literally walk on the heads of his subjects!
Ha, ha! And if he didn't enjoy doing that,
    I can think of plenty of people who would, can't you?
Indeed, there is another type of American who not only
        visits Italy but also writes poems about the place in which
we, the readers, are made to feel like ostlers or bootblacks
        or street sweepers on whom they, the lordly, step from
one palace to another, never soiling the hems of their silken gowns
        as they tread unthinkingly on such human cobblestones as we,

    and here I remember what my student Ron Jenkins wrote
about just such a poet who had written just such a poem,
        that is, "As a gay man from desperately poor circumstances,
I get bored—even angry—very easily at the lives
        of literate, affluent, heterosexual bourgeoisie,
especially those with the means to loll around piazzas."
        Ha! Ron, I too hate the fuckers, and I hereby resolve
never to be one. That is, I can't help being literate
        and heterosexual, but I'll never be affluent,

    and, try as I may, I've never been able to loll,
either in the personal or the poetic sense, and it is perhaps
        because of this very physical ungainliness that I also like,
as a sort of frame around one's personal world, not only a *corridoio*
        or corridor but also the *chiostro* or cloister
that's found at the heart of every monastery so the holy fathers
        of this or that order will have a place to walk and praise God
for His generosity in giving them not only soft breezes and flowers
        and birdsong but also their own sins to contemplate,

    as well as a *studiolo,* or—well, there's no one-word translation
for this term meaning "phone-booth-sized reading room
        with elaborate wood inlay and other fine appointments
intended to inspire deep philosophical thought
        on the part of a nobleperson, generally a duke,
who repairs there when in need of such rumination."
        Corridoio, chiostro, studiolo: snug spaces,
tiny hidey-holes in a world too big for its own good,
        refuges from the sun or from assassins.

Why, they are like the shapes of pasta or of little cookies,
some like ears, others like pens or butterflies.
Mr. Wordsworth said nuns fret not at their narrow cells
nor poets within the confines of their sonnets.
Though I have to say I was just a tad discomfited
the other day: as I was looking through an iron gate
at the very pretty Chiostro degli Aranci in the Badia Fiorentina,
a man comes up and stands right behind me—
as in, not merely close to or near me, but *right behind* me,

his toes teaching my heels, his breath warm on my neck.
Now who is this guy, you are asking yourself:
an associate professor of art history? My alter ego? A rogue monk
like the one in *The Marble Faun*? A German?
And these, of course, are precisely the same questions
I am asking myself! But when I turn to look at him,
I see he is a midwesterner, from Dayton or Cleveland, say,
or better yet, from Cincinnati, the only U.S. city
named for a secret society!

He is a large, rumpled man
and he smiles at me, though sadly, and I wonder
if he isn't the kind of guy who, when he gets off work,
dresses up as a clown and goes to cheer up sick kids
in the hospitals there in the Cincinnati area,
but now he's looking out at the garden with the well
at its center and he's thinking of his own mortality,
and he knows that, in a few hours,
the Benedictine monks will be walking around

this same cloister after dinner and thinking about something
very similar, although in his imagination
he sees them not as monks but as clowns, big solemn guys
with baggy pants and big orange tufts of hair and bright red noses,
and they clasp their hands behind their backs
and they look at the ground as they shuffle along,
their size 30 shoes slapping the terrazzo,
and they're thinking, Life's pretty terrible—
well, no, not really, not when you think about it.

Lame as a Robin

The cumulative ticket is nominative and it can be used within three days.
On the ticket is showed an entrance time table: this time table is indicative.
—on the back of a ticket to the Uffizi

Halfway across the piazza, I turn to wave at Barbara,
and she says, "Don't forget to buy some Tenderly!"
because in Italy we have the habit of calling products
by their brand names, not only to create a third language
in addition to our native tongue and that of the locals
but also to avoid such vulgar public reminders
as "Don't forget to buy some toilet paper!"
so that milk is Mukki, facial tissue becomes Tempo,
laundry detergent is now Cocolino, and so on,

and as I stand waving the way a beauty queen
taught me once, my hand not flopping up and down
like a catfish out of water but swinging back and forth
the way you'd do if you were trying to unscrew the lid
of a family-size jar of mayonnaise, I can't help thinking,
first, of the little neighborhood boy who thought
that the Broadway musical was called *Lame as a Robin,*
its connotation of injured innocence at least as expressive as,
if not more so than, Monsieur Hugo's original title,

and then, in quick succession, of that guy Ragnor asking me
Do you say, "I hate French" or "I hate the French?"
and me saying, "The French!" and him asking,
Is it, "You are sweetheart" or "You are the sweetheart?"
and me saying, It's either "You're a sweetheart"
or "You're my sweetheart," and him saying, What is difference?
and then asking, Is it "I study maths" or "I study the maths?"
and me saying, "I study maths," though we don't say "maths"
in this country! and him saying, Why not?

and me saying, Because we're not English!
and him saying, This what we speak is not the English?
Then how do you call what is it what we speak?
and me saying, It's English, it just isn't English English,
and him saying, Okay, we forget about this one,

let me ask you instead if we say "I eat beans"
or "I eat the beans?" and me saying, It's "I eat beans"
        if that's all there is but "I eat the beans" if you eat the beans
                instead of the peas and him saying, I don't see difference,

                and it occurs to me that if the world depended
        on our precise description of it for its existence,
                it would be a spotty patch, indeed, consisting
of little more than childhood memories, a clutch
        of keen resentments, and a vague sense of our last few meals.
                On the one hand, we do not wish to find ourselves in
the position of the bewildered older female relative who looked
                at the menu in the trendy restaurant and said, How do you know
                what to order when you don't know what anything is,

                just as we don't want to become such misguided champions
        of clarity that we find ourselves in the position
                of the commentators on Homer and Aristotle
in *Gulliver's Travels* who are forced to keep their distance
                in the underworld "through a consciousness of Shame
                        and Guilt, because they had so horribly represented
the Meaning of those Authors to Posterity,"
        remembering that if the great tragedy of science
                is that a beautiful hypothesis can be slain by an ugly fact,

                as Thomas Huxley said, so is it equally certain
        that a beautiful reality can be reduced to a pile of rubbish
                by the application of some slipshod language, like a coat
of naval-issue battleship-gray paint on a fine old Tuscan table.
        Meanwhile, no one in the piazza is giving any indication
                that they are in the least bit aware of what we say or do,
lost as they are in their own search for personal-care products,
        their brains humming with code, the specks and flashes
                that make a phrase, a memory, the face of someone they love.

Letters to Juliet

When Barbara calls from Verona, she says
they're looking for a woman to answer
        all the letters addressed to Juliet Capulet,
because the woman who's answered them for years
        is tired of the *problemi di cuore* and wants to retire.
Problems of the heart: these, at least, haven't changed.

        In the Dark Ages of my own life,
I had fantasies of myself as a swashbuckler,
        stuffing my pouch with the gems I'd sucked
from the navels of dusky maidens,
        though my search for amorous adventures
just lead me into one utterly inappropriate relationship

        after another, such as the one with the woman
who claimed she could make people disappear completely
        except for their eyes. And that's love, sure,
though love's also Pepi Deutsch hoarding three slices
        of bread and slathering them with marmalade
so she can make her daughter Clara

        a 17th-birthday cake in the hell of Auschwitz-Birkenau.
And it's 50-year-old Antonio Delfini opening the bier
        of his father, who had died when he was 30, and weeping
as he gazes at the body of a man 20 years younger than himself.
        Now who was he loving, his father or himself?
Surely both, for while we love those we love

        almost with all our hearts, we love ourselves even more,
which means we pity ourselves even more,
        as I do now, for instance, because while I'm grateful
for the silence in which to read and write for hours on end,
        I can't help thinking, from time to time, that one day
this room will be forever silent except for the sound of one person

        making coffee or pressing the collar of an old shirt,
and that person could be either of us—
        unless one day we're in our eighties, say, on a flight to,

oh, I don't know, Prague, and we have a couple of icy martinis
        on the tray tables in front of us, and one seat over,
this nervous guy opens his carry-on bag, and inside it there's this bomb . . .

        Maybe all love is self-love.
Maybe, when the *New York Times* food critic said the best Wiener schnitzel
        he ever had wasn't all that much different from
the worst Wiener schnitzel he ever had,
        he meant that, taken as individuals, we are all too much
like Wiener schnitzel—too schnitzel-y, in a word.

        Last night, as I sat in the piazza, I thought of Barbara,
and as people opened and closed their shutters and lighted up
        this room and darkened that one, I pretended
all the little flashes were the eyes of those who had disappeared
        and who'd come back to look for someone,
though who it was, they couldn't remember.

A Man Like You but Older

Here's how you find a really good restaurant:
you go to the part of town where you want to eat,
    then you stand around till you see someone
who looks like you, or a slightly better-fed version of yourself,
        maybe, someone just a little paunchier
than you are and a year or two older and certainly
    someone more affluent than you but not much,
because after all you're thinking ahead here,

    you're looking for the person you'll be in a couple
of years, the one who *really* knows where to go
        and what to get, not the person you are now, for as much
as you love yourself, it goes without saying
        that in the future you expect to be someone
you love even more, someone you absolutely worship,
    a person you'd spend every waking moment
with if you weren't that person already.

    You certainly don't want to accost the person
you'll be in 20 years! This one is liable
    to be stove up from excesses or, by the same token,
puritanical and disapproving, a regular Savonarola,
        or maybe just someone with whom you
no longer share—I mean, don't yet share—
    enough common cultural references and therefore
with whom you can no more converse

    than I might with the self I was 27 years ago
behind the shuttered windows of the *casa di cura*
        on the Via Pietro Thouar where I stood just this afternoon,
brushing back my graying hair and squinting to see
        inside the delivery room where my younger self
wheels and holds his head in his hands and tries
    not to weep with rage and frustration: my son Will
has just been born and he isn't breathing,

    and the Italian doctor and the nurses have taken him
into another room, and I'm afraid they're going to
        bring him back dead, and my then-wife is sleeping

like a baby herself, though her blood is everywhere,
         and there's no one for me to talk to, and I'm afraid
they're going to come in and hand me this dead child
         and say *Mi dispiace tanto,* and I'll say I'm sorry, too,
and then what will I say, and to whom?

         The man I finally ask about the restaurant
is a dreamy sort who is licking an ice-cream cone
         with an air of more than just a little self-satisfaction
and who answers my query with a restrained enthusiasm
         that I find charming now that I'm sitting with Barbara
in the place he recommended and waiting
         for what promises to be some excellent roast fish,
grilled vegetables, and cold wine to arrive

         and remembering how unhappy my younger self was,
the self with darker hair and perfect eyesight
         but no real worldly experience of any kind,
yet I thought I was the oldest man in the world,
         though I was just 27 myself.
And just then a nurse comes back with Will in her arms,
         and he looks like any other baby, like
a bewildered mushroom, and she hands him to me,

         and I feel his breath on my cheek, and for a moment
I am frozen, still petrified by the horror of everything
         that had almost happened, and then suddenly
something goes off inside my chest like a nova exploding
         and I feel all this *love* for the infant Will Kirby,
this bawling bunch of wrinkled protoplasm,
         but that was 27 years ago, and now Will is himself
a doctor, an American one: he started breathing

         there in Florence and kept at it and came home
in a little sling and not a coffin and drank his milk
         and ate his mashed bananas and went to school
and to med school and is himself now bringing babies back to life,
         their fathers as crazy with fear as I that day—
how I wish I had walked over and thrown back
         the shutters and looked out the window and seen
my older self there on the sidewalk, smiling and waving.

The Little Sisters of the Sacred Heart

I'm bouncing across the Scottish heath in a rented Morris Minor
          and listening to an interview with Rat Scabies, drummer
of the first punk band, The Damned, and Mr. Scabies,
          who's probably 50 or so and living comfortably on royalties,
is as recalcitrant as ever, as full of despair and self-loathing,

but the interviewer won't have it, and he keeps calling him "Rattie,"
          saying, "Ah, Rattie, it's all a bit of a put-on, isn't it?"
and "Ah, you're just pulling the old leg now, aren't you, Rattie?"
          to which Mr. Scabies keeps saying things like
"We're fooked, ya daft prat. Oh, yeah, absolutely—fooked!"

Funny old Rattie—he believed in nothing, which is something.
          If it weren't for summat, there'd be naught, as they say
in that part of the world. I wonder if his dad wasn't a bit of a bastard,
          didn't drink himself to death, say, as opposed to a dad like mine,
who, though also dead now, was as nice as he could be when he was alive.

A month before, I'd been in Florence and walked by the *casa di cura* where
          my son Will was born 27 years ago, though it's not a hospital
now but a home for the old nuns of Le Suore Minime del Sacra Cuore
          who helped to deliver and bathe and care for him when he was just
a few minutes old, and when I look over the gate, I see three

of these holy sisters sitting in the garden there, and I wave at them,
          and they wave back, and I wonder if they were on duty
when Will was born, these women who have had no sex at all,
          probably not even very much candy, yet who believe in something
that may be nothing, after all, though I love them for giving me my boy.

They're dozing and talking, these mystical brides of Christ,
          and thinking about their Husband, and it looks to me
as though they're having their version of the *sacra conversazione,*
          a favorite subject of Renaissance artists in which people who care
for one another are painted chatting together about noble things,

and I'm wondering if, as I walk by later when the shadows are long,
          their white faces will be like stars against their black habits,
the three of them a constellation about to rise into the vault
          that arches over Tuscany, the fires there now twinkling,
now steadfast in the chambered heart of the sky.

Guy walks into his doctor's office and tells the doctor that he's been feeling really bad lately and asks if there is anything the doctor can do to help. The doctor tells him that he can run a few tests and tells the man to come back in a week. A week later, the guy comes back and says, "Well, Doc, what's the verdict?" The doctor replies, "It doesn't look good; you don't have very long to live." The guy gets a very frightened look on his face and asks, "Well, how long do I have to live?" The doctor responds with "Ten." Naturally the guy is angry: "Ten what? Weeks? Months?" The doctor then continues, "Nine, " and the guy says "Nine? I thought you just said ten!" The doctor says, "Eight."

After sitting a little while, Miss Crawford was up again. "I must move," said she, "resting fatigues me. I have looked across the ha-ha till I am weary. I must go and look through that iron gate at the same view, without being able to see it so well."

— JANE AUSTEN, *Mansfield Park*

Looking for Percy Sledge

Guy's telling me he and his buddy are driving around Atlanta
    one night in the seventies and they hear the DJ say,
"Percy Sledge is in town for just one more night, folks,
    and he's staying in room such-and-such at the so-and-so motel
and would like all of his fans to come on out and see him,"
    and they're thinking, Percy Sledge hasn't had
much radio play lately (and won't again until 1987 when
    Oliver Stone puts his only big hit on the *Platoon* soundtrack),

and while Mr. Sledge might have another type of fan in mind
    altogether, my friend and his buddy go to the motel
and knock on the door, and this chubby guy with a gap in his teeth
    and this wild hair invites them in, asks them to sit down,
offers them a soft drink, and the three of them talk
    for a while about music, sure, but also about sports and food,
and then the two men get up to go, and the guy
    shakes their hands and thanks them for stopping by,

and just then my friend stops to take a sip in the middle of his tale,
    and for no real reason I can think of,
I recall the most beautiful first sentence of any story
    ever written, Poe's "Fall of the House of Usher,"
which begins:"During the whole of a dull, dark, and soundless day
    in the autumn of the year, when the clouds hung
oppressively low in the heavens, I had been passing alone,
    on horseback, through a singularly dreary tract of country."

Lovely, huh? It's the word "heavens" that makes it so:
    everything here on earth is dull, dark, soundless,
autumnal, oppressive and low, but it's better up there—in the heavens!
    In the place where Roderick and Madeleine Usher will go
and where Poe himself will join them in a few short years.
    Oh, and the verb tenses, especially the "had been"!
For if the speaker were miserable then, is it not likely
    that he is happy now? Even if he isn't.

It is language to dance to, is it not,
    to waltz to, one might say, and slowly, soberly, like bears,
not wildly like frenzied chickens:

Flaubert said language is a cracked kettle
on which we beat out tunes for bears to dance to,
    while all the time we long to move the stars to pity—
but we *are* bears, are we not, lumbering about
    to the harsh clang of the quotidian?

For Wittgenstein, philosophical problems
    are "language on vacation," by which he meant—
well, I'm not sure. How about this: philosophical or,
    for my purpose, poetical language, is language on vacation
from humdrum usages, from weather reports and office memos.
    Think of nouns and verbs in lounge chairs, basking under
a tropical sun as their paper-umbrellaed drinks grow watery
    yet somehow even more intoxicating.

Here's a good word: "isthmus." It would make a fine title
    for a book, though not one of mine. And "Zamboni":
now there's a fun yet a deeply responsible word,
    with its connotations of erasure, of wiping clean, of virtue.
Charles Ives loved virtue; Harold C. Schonberg said
    Charles Ives "yearned for the virtues of an older, town-meeting,
village-band, transcendentalist, Emersonian America,"
    though he expressed those yearnings "in the most advanced,

unorthodox, ear-splitting, grating music composed by anybody
    anywhere up to that time." Ives let the notes go out for a walk,
didn't he, as did musicians as different as Jim Morrison and Poulenc,
    now buried together in Père Lachaise. Oh, and the two guys,
the other two: the one's telling me they're standing in the parking lot
    thinking, Was that really Percy Sledge, and they look back,
and suddenly the guy throws his arms out wide and sings,
    "When a mannn loves a womannnn . . ."

Public Idiot

There's a kind of reason that transcends logic,
        if you catch my drift: "I'm going to hang myself
from that branch right there," Maureen said,
        "and shine a spotlight on the body,"
and when Daphne came home that evening,
        there was Maureen, twisting slowly in the beam.

When my Will was 12, I took him to Sears to buy a Lego,
        and when I hurried him, he said,
"Don't rush me, Dad, this is probably the last toy
        I'll ever buy." How did he know that—
how do we know anything? How did people know
        they were living in the Dark Ages, or did they?

When I was his age, my mom and dad took me
        and my brother out west one summer and we crossed
these fields of amber waving grain with pollen so thick
        you could part it like curtains,
and I began to wheeze, so my mother wet a hanky
        and said "Here, tie this across your face,"

and I said, "What, and look like a public idiot,"
        and she said, "No, a cowboy," though later
people were laughing at me at a gas station,
        which is when I saw my brother had printed the words
PUBLIC IDIOT on a piece of paper
        and stuck it in the car's rear window.

Point: who cares? I'd been a hero
        in my own mind the whole time,
and you never know what someone else
        is thinking unless you are that person,
which you can't be, and who would want to anyway?
        It's enough of a job to be ourselves.

Friend of mine finds out he has exactly the same
        blood chemistry as his father, who died younger
than he is now, so he explains to his kids

that Dad'll die if they can't start eating more fish
and less pizza, and the kids are sweet, they love Dad,
        but they say, "Nope, sorry, pizza it is."

I mean, they won't even let him have anchovies!
        And they're not bad kids,
it's not that they want him to die:
        they just know that if they say okay to the fish,
it'll be halibut, mackerel, pike, tuna,
        snapper, grouper, mullet, scrod, catfish,

codfish, bluefish, and swordfish every night
        until they go away to college,
because Dad doesn't care
        how nasty his dinner is, he just wants to live!
The kids are being themselves, which is their job:
        they know if they say "No fish,"

clever Dad will come up with
        some third plan the way he always does
when he and Mom can't agree where to go
        for vacation or even what movie
to take everybody to on Sunday,
        like maybe pizza for them and fish for him and Mom,

even though they also know he wants
        the whole family to eat the same thing,
to be like a real family that way,
        an old-fashioned family passing platters
around the table and talking and laughing together
        instead of a modern family

with morose kids shoving these cheesy wedges
        into their cakeholes while Mom and Dad
pull the skin off their salmon or extract
        the needle-thin bones, figuring what profiteth it
a man to save his heart
        if he end up with a punctured esophagus?

Another friend told me the star quarterback
        of the Cairo Syrupmakers quit football
in his junior year so he could smoke cigarettes,

and now everybody in Cairo is talking
about how stupid he is, how unsportsmanlike,
    though he knows the right thing

for him at this moment is to smoke those ciggies,
    and who's to say he shouldn't?
Every fall, someone breaks his neck
    on the football field.
And Maureen, she'd thought about her death so long—
    surely she'd told herself, "Look, it's a free country."

Calling Robert Bly

We're reading "In Danger from the Outer World"
in my graduate seminar and somebody asks,
          "I know what all the bad stuff in the poem is—
the fire, the water, the plane crash, the grave—
          but what's this 'shining thing' inside us
that 'shakes its bamboo bars'?" and I say,

          "Umm, the unconscious mind?" and somebody else says,
"Maybe it's the soul," and a fourth person sneers
          and says, "A poet like Robert Bly wouldn't believe
in a stupid idea like that," and the third person
          says, "You're not Robert Bly, how do you know
what Robert Bly believes?" and the fourth says,

          "You're not me, how do you know what I know?"
so to keep the peace, I interrupt with
          the standard English professor's joke:
"Hey, too bad we can't just call the poet up
          and ask him what he meant, huh?"
and then I think, Wait a minute,

          we're not talking about Wordsworth here,
and since it's break time anyway,
          I say, "Okay, everybody, come on up
to my office, we're gonna call Robert Bly!"
          and I leg it upstairs with my students
shuffling along behind and grab my copy

          of the *Directory of American Poets* and sure enough,
there's a Robert Bly in a town called Moose Lake,
          Minnesota, and I dial the number,
and a woman answers, and I say, "Can I speak
          to Robert Bly!" and she says, "Just a minute!"
and then this voice says, "Hello!"

          and I say, "Mr. Bly?" and the voice at the other end says, "Yes?"
and I introduce myself and we chat a bit and then
          I tell him we're reading this poem of his

called "In Danger from the Outer World,"
        only nobody gets this one image, and can he
explain it to us, and he says, "Aw, you know!

        It's the soul or the human spirit—something like that!"
I turn to the students, but by this time most of them
        have drifted away to the bathroom or the coffee machine,
so I cover the receiver and say to no one,
        "Mr. Bly says I'm right—it is the unconscious mind!"
and I look out the window as far as I can

        and imagine Robert Bly sitting there with his phone in his hand
and all of America between us, the line
        going out through Benevolence, Georgia, where a woman
who has just finished baking a buttermilk pie
        for a family dinner the next day
decides it isn't enough and starts to make a second;

        then on to Difficult, Tennessee, where one man
has just sold his car to another and is now taking
        a photo of the new owner alongside his new vehicle;
then Knob Lick, Kentucky, where a man is having sex
        with a woman who is younger than he is
and doesn't love him anymore, though she hasn't told him yet;

        and Goreville, Illinois,
where two men tell a third they're going to whip his ass,
        and he startles them when he shrugs and says,
"Go ahead"; and then Vesper, Wisconsin,
        where a child is dying of acute myeloid leukemia,
and his parents can't do a thing about it.

        In the darkness outside Robert Bly's cabin, a moose
is cropping ferns, his leathery flap of an upper lip
        closing over the fronds as delicately
as a lady's hand picking up a tea cake,
        and he looks up, startled, when Robert Bly
laughs at something I've said, and then

        Robert Bly says, "How are your students—are they any good?"
and I say, "They are, though they seem
        a little tired tonight," and he says,

"Are they good writers?" and I say,
         "Yeah, most of them," and he says,
"How about you—you a writer?"

    and whatever I say makes Mr. Bly laugh again really loudly,
but this time the moose just keeps on eating,
         finishing its little patch of ostrich ferns
and sniffing the night air and thinking, Umm—asparagus!
         and then stepping off, graceful as a skater,
toward the lake it can't see but knows is there.

On My Mother's Blindness

Ninety-five and blind, my mother is doing
her fabulous imitation of Cousin Rack
        sobbing in the back of the church
as his estranged daughter gets married,
        Cousin Rack being this abusive drunk

famous already in my family for two other stories,
        the first involving his attempt to run down
these swans in his power boat and hitting a stump
        and having to swim to shore, his beautiful craft
heading for the bottom as the swans look on serenely,

        and the second being the time he chased
his mother-in-law, Aunt Gin, around the sofa
        with the butcher knife, too drunk to catch her,
which at least some in the family seem to regret,
        though neither of these tales appeals to my mom

as much as the one she is telling now
        of the exiled Rack, banned from all gatherings,
living alone in well-heeled alcoholic squalor,
        and creeping into the church to see
his only daughter given away by her granddad,

        Uncle Dick, Aunt Gin's husband, and then losing it,
his red face turning crimson as he throws back
        his head and goes—and here my mother twists
her face up like his—"uh-hoo-hoo-HOO-HOO-HOO!!"
        How happy she is! How malicious! How she enjoys

her own malice, and the rest of us, too,
        for she *will* see Cousin Rack's well-earned misery,
will make us see it, too. How I love her
        when I think how much of my childhood I spent
in bed, reading and glancing down the hall

        to the kitchen where I'd see her cooking
or marking her students' papers or just

sitting at the table thinking—about what?
My brother, maybe, and the gloom that grew
        in him until, one day, it suddenly vanished forever.

Or my father and his cooling love. Or me:
        if I'd been a mail-order child, there were
so many things wrong with me—asthma, allergies,
        polio, chronic self-pity persisting to this day—
that another mother would have sent me back.

        My mother is the best storyteller I know,
and I thought of her in Paris when I read
            that the great French poet Jacques Prévert
saw this beggar who had a sign that said,
        "Blind Man Without a Pension,"

and when he asked the beggar how he was doing,
        the beggar said, "Oh, very badly. People just
pass by and drop nothing in my hat, the swine,"
        so Prévert said, "Here, give me that placard,"
and, passing by a few days later, asked again

        how things were going, and the beggar
said, "Fantastic! My hat fills up
            three times a day," and that was because,
on the back of his placard, Prévert had written,
        "Spring is coming, but I won't see it."

My mother is her own great French poet.
        Rack's tears leap from her sightless face
as she tells her story—though when he was found dead
        and so covered with mold "at first they thought
he was a black man," I remember her weeping.

France / Francine's Begonias

Just before we move into Pascal and Francine's apartment,
    Francine shows us how to work the washer
and fax machine and then asks us to water her begonias,

saying they need a bottle of Evian water every day,
    and I'm thinking, Evian? Still,
we want to impress these people, to rent the apartment

from them again, maybe, plus Matisse's grandson
    lives in the building and so does
Adrian Lyne, who directed *Fatal Attraction* and *Lolita*,

and for all I know they give their plants mineral water,
    so I say, sure, whatever you say, even though
I think, Hell, I'll just use tap water, she'll never know,

but on the way over to the restaurant, Pascal tells me
    Francine uses mineral water for *everything*,
she even dumps two of those big liter-and-a-half bottles

of Evian in the pasta pot before she makes spaghetti,
    and I say, That's some nutritious spaghetti,
and he says, Yeah, but lugging all those bottles upstairs

is a killer, and I'm thinking, Okay, Evian water it is,
    but I'm thinking also how funny it is that
people as cosmopolitan and well-off as Pascal and Francine

are up there at night boiling water for pasta, just like
    me and Barbara! The nearest place
to get water is this store the size of a phone booth

that's one street over, and whenever I ask for something,
    like vinegar, say, the monsieur who owns it
always wriggles out from behind his counter and stands

in the middle of the store with his hands on his hips
    and his elbows touching the walls and says,
"Heinnn, du vinaiiiigre" and takes 15 minutes to find it,

and the Evian water, too, is in a new place every week,
    and the guy says, "Heinnn, de l'eau Eviannn,"
and after three weeks I've had it up to here dragging

all that Evian upstairs for Francine's stupid begonias!
    Not to mention how expensive it is.
They're in the south of France, are Pascal and Francine,

and I'm thinking, Must be nice, having two houses
    and rental income and people
to keep an eye on things and pamper your begonias,

treating them better than all dogs and most people,
    while you swan about and look at
the cave paintings at Lascaux in the Périgord, though

before you exchange the soft light of the Dordogne for
    the hissing carbide lamps that reveal to you
the unicorn and the Chinese horse of the Main Chamber,

you stop first at the little town of Montignac for
    La Galette de Pommes de Terre au Chevre
en Salade followed by Le Navarin d'Agneau Printanier

and, for dessert, Les Pots de Crème au Chocolat.
    Then it's off to the chateau of Lascaux,
high above the valley of the Vézère, property of

the Comtesse de la Rochefoucauld-Montbel, née Darbley,
    to see the celebrated paintings,
having bypassed those in the Pech' Merle cave at Cabrerets

and those in the cave of Font de Gaume at Les Eyzies,
    though not missing out on your fair share of
Les Compotiers de Boeuf à la Parisienne, La Blanquette de

Jarret de Veau, La Salade des Oranges au Sorbet Chocolat—
    or is it La Terrine de Foie
au Volaille Campagnarde, Le Maquereau Frais au Poivre Vert,

and La Crême Brulée à la Cassonade? My faith, either
    it is the Pomerol and the Margaux
you've drunk or else it is the heady prospect of traversing

the Axial Passage to see its deer with gigantic antlers,
        its tawny horses, and its red cows
with truncated-conical muzzles, for here you're likely

to recall Les Huitres Chaudes aux Endive you enjoyed earlier
        as well as La Fricassée de Canard aux
Haricots Blancs and La Crêpe Soufflé au Coulis d'Abricot,

otherwise known as zuh oyster, zuh duck, and zuh pancake.
        Or perhaps it is the anxiety you will feel
upon emerging once more into the soft light of the Dordogne

to meet not only the Comtesse de la Rochefoucauld-Montbel,
        née Darbley, but also the Abbé Breuil,
foremost living expert on the caves. What will you say to

such luminaries? I know: you'll greet them in their native
        tongue. Bonjour, Madame la Comtesse! Salut,
Monsieur l'Abbé! Join us in a Filet de Saumon Fumé Mariné.

You are going to have that and then a Turbot Grillé
        au Beurre Blanc, followed by cheese this time
and fruit: Roquefort, Brie, Camembert, and Port Salut,

pommes, figues, ananas, cerises. You'll drink a Puligny-
        Montrachet and toast the men and women of the
Pleistocene or Ice Age, your Upper Paleolithic ancestors

who lived, not in some older aspect of this world with
        its sleepy little town of Montignac
that seems always to have been here, but in another world

altogether, dead now these two hundred centuries.
        You will have the big fun!
How you will quaff the Armagnac, the Calvados, the

Eau de Vie Poire William in honor of artistry unsurpassed!
        And then you will reflect,
in whatever language best suits such activity,

that if France is synonymous with "richness of freedoms,"
        the greatest of which is your own freedom
in choosing among them, then France is many things,

is music, for example, is choosing between Gustav Mahler
        and Burt Bacharach. Or Ella Fitzgerald
and Jacques Brel. Or Gabriel Fauré and John Lee Hooker—

or all six! Or books or paintings or statues or movies.
        Or books *and* paintings *and* statues *and* movies.
And music. Alors, there has to be more to life than life.

In October, Francine calls from Aix. She says, "I think
        maybe you figure this out on your own,
but my English sometimes she is not quite so good,

and Pascal have me worry, so I tell you I don't mean
        a bottle of Evian water every day
but an Evian bottle of water! Every day, though."

So the Evian *bottle,* but . . . okay, I get it, and say,
        "How is it there in the south?"
and Francine says, "Okay, though not so much to do—

Paris is better, hein? Plus the car, she break down,
        and Pascal is not fix." Francine
is not in France, in other words. And the cave people,

where were they? Not much to do there, either, though
        they didn't know that. So they were
in France, yeah, though they wouldn't have used that name.

The Search for Baby Combover

In Paris one night the doorbell rings,
        and there's this little guy, shaking like a leaf
and going "uh-uh-uh-UNH-ah!" and his eyes get big
                and he raises his hands like a gospel singer
and goes "UNH-ah-uh-uh-uh-UNH-uh-ah!"

and for just a fraction of a second I think
        he's doing the first part of Wilson Pickett's
"Land of a Thousand Dances" and that he wants me
                to join him in some kind of weird welcome
to the neighborhood, so I raise my hands a little

and begin to sort of hum along, though
        not very loudly in case I'm wrong about this,
and I'm smiling the way old people smile
                when they can't hear you but want you to know
that everything's okay as far as they're concerned

or a poet smiles in a roomful of scientists,
        as if to say, "Hey! I'm just a poet!
But your stuff's great, really! Even if
                I don't understand any of it!" And by the time
I start to half-wonder if this gentleman wants me

to take the you-got-to-know-how-to-pony part
        or means to launch into it himself, he gives
a little hop and slaps his hands down to his sides
                and says, "PLEASE! YOU MUST NOT MOVE
THE FURNITURE AFTER ELEVEN O'CLOCK OF THE NIGHT!"

so I lower my own hands and say, "Whaaaa . . . ?"
        and he says, "ALWAYS YOU ARE MOVING IT WHEN
THE BABY TRY TO SLEEP! YOU MUST NOT DO IT!"
                And now that he's feeling a little bolder,
he steps in closer, where the light's better,

and I see he's got something on his head,
        like strands of oily seaweed, something

you'd expect to find on a rock after one of
          those big tanker spills in the Channel,
so I lean a little bit and realize it's what

stylists call a "combover," not a bad idea
          on the tall fellows but definitely a grooming no-no
for your vertically challenged caballeros,
          of which Monsieur here is certainly one,
especially if they are yelling at you.

But I'd read an article about AA that said
          when your loved ones stage an intervention
and go off on you for getting drunk
          and busting up the furniture and running out
into traffic and threatening to kill the President,

it's better to just let them wind down
          and then say, "You're probably right,"
because if you're combative, they will be, too,
          and then your problems will just start over again,
so I wait till Mr. Combover stops shaking—

it's not nice, I know, but it's the first name that comes to mind—
          and I say, "You're probably right," and he raises
a finger and opens his mouth as if to say something
          but then snaps his jaw shut and whirls around
and marches downstairs, skidding a little

and windmilling his arms and almost falling
          but catching himself, though not without
that indignant backward glance we all give
          the stupid step that some stupid idiot would have
attended to long ago if he hadn't been so stupid.

The next day, I ask Nadine the *gardienne*
          qu'est-ce que c'est the deal *avec* the *monsieur*
qui lives under *moi,* and Nadine says his *femme*
          is *toujours* busting his chops, but *il est* afraid
of her, so *il* takes out his *rage* on the rest of *nous.*

There's something else, though: a few days later,
          Barbara and I see Mr. and Mrs. Combover

crossing the Pont Marie, and she is a virtual giantess
        compared to him! Now I remember once hearing Barbara
give boyfriend advice to this niece of mine,

and Barbara said (1) he's got to have a job,
        (2) he's got to tell you you're beautiful all the time,
and (3) he's got to be taller than you are,
        so when I see Mrs. Combover looming over her hubby,
I think, Well, that explains the busted chops.

Not only that, Mrs. Combover looks cheap.
        She looks rich, sure—Nadine had told me *Monsieur*
is some *sorte de* diplomat *avec* the Chilean delegation—
        but also like one of those professional ladies
offering her services up around the Rue St. Denis.

But who are they, really? "Combover" is one
        of those names from a fifties black-and-white movie;
he's the kind of guy neighborhood kids call "Mr. C."
        and who has a boss who says things like, "Now see here,
Combover, this sort of thing just won't do!"

He's like one of Dagwood's unnamed colleagues—
        he's not even Dagwood, who at least excites
Mr. Dithers enough to be fired a couple
        of times a week, not to mention severely beaten.
Only Dagwood is really in charge. Everything goes his way!

Despite chronic incompetence, ol' Dag keeps
        the job that allows him his fabulous home life:
long naps, towering sandwiches, affectionate
        and well-behaved teenaged children, a loyal dog,
and, best of all, the love of Blondie.

Blondie! The name says it all: glamorous but fun.
        Big trashy Mrs. Combover is not glamorous,
although she thinks she is, and no fun at all.
        She is the anti-Blondie. Her job seems to be
to stay home and smoke, since we're always smelling

the cigarette fumes that seep up through the floor
        into our apartment day and night. And he says

we're keeping Baby Combover awake when we move
        the furniture, which we've never done, but then
we've never seen Baby Combover, either. Or heard him.

Baby Combover: the world's first silent baby.
        Barbara has this theory that, after a life
of prostitution, Mrs. Combover has not only repented but
                undergone a false pregnancy and imaginary birth.
Therefore, the reason why Baby Combover is silent

is that he is not a real baby who fusses and eats and
        wets and poops but is instead a pillowcase with knots
for ears and a smiley-face drawn with a Magic Marker and
                a hole for its mouth so Mrs. Combover can teach it
to smoke when it's older, like eight, say.

Now I know what they fight about: "You never spend
        any time with the baby!" hisses Mrs. Combover.
"I will—later, when he can talk!" says Mr. Combover.
                "Here I am stuck with this baby all day long!
And those horrible people upstairs!"

And he says, "Oh, be silent, you . . . prostitute!"
        And she says, "Quiet, you horrible man—
not in front of the baby!" Maybe it's time
        for a call to the police. Or the newspapers.
I can see the headlines now: OÙ EST L'ENFANT COMBOVER?

I feel sorry for him. With parents like this,
        it would be better if someone were to kidnap him.
Or I could take him back to America with me,
        I who have a wife who loves me and two grown sons.
Why not? We've got all this extra room now.

We'll feed him a lot and tickle him;
        there's nothing funnier than a fat, happy baby.
And when the boys come home to visit,
        they'll take him out with them in their sports cars:
"It's my little brother!" they'll say. "He's French!"

The neighborhood kids, once a band of sullen mendicants,
        will beg us to let him play with them,

even though he doesn't speak their language.
      Look! There they go toward the baseball field,
with Baby Combover under their arm!

I love you, Baby Combover! You *are* Joseph Campbell's
      classic mythical hero, i.e., "an agent of change
who relinquishes self-interest and breaks down
      the established social order." But you're so pale!
You've stayed out too long and caught cold.

Barbara and the boys gather around his bed;
      they hug each other, and we try not to cry.
Baby Combover is smiling—he always smiled, that kid.
      His little mouth begins to move, and we lean in
and think we hear him say, "Be bwave fo' me . . ."

Back in Paris, Mr. Combover grows a full head of hair.
      Mrs. Combover reaches up to touch it.
He puts down his attaché case and caresses her cheek.
      "How beautiful you are!" he says. It's so quiet now.
Then they hear it: in the next room, a child is crying.

The Elephant of the Sea

Because I make the big bucks fooling around
with words, in France sometimes I like to say
        "Sylvia Plath" instead of "s'il vous plaît,"
as when I open the door for Barbara and say,
        "Après-vous, Sylvia Plath!" But yesterday
the lady in the boulangerie asked me what I wanted,
        and I said, "Une baguette, Sylvia Plath! Crap . . ."

Before I move to France, I have to help
my friend *from* France buy his first American automobile,
        and naturally he wants everything on his car
to be just like mine, right down to the manatee on the tag,
        for which I pay an extra seventeen dollars that
goes into some kind of special fund for endangered species.
        He says, "You have zuh elephant of zuh sea

on your matriculation?" Tag, I say, tag!
And manatee! which is a Native American word meaning, uh,
        l'elephant de mer, and no, you don't want it,
because we're trying to save money here, remember?
        We go over this several times, yet when we are in
the tag office and I am filling out a form to have his title
        sent to my address, I hear Antoine say,

"I can have zuh elephant of zuh sea
on my matriculation?" to a clerk who's got this grin
        on her face like she's either seeing God
or having an aneurysm, and I can see she loves it,
        she's going to tell the women she goes fishing with
on Lake Jackson about this foreign fellow,
        nice as he could be, though, who comes into

the office the other day, and says, "elephant of
zuh sea" and "matriculation," and they'll say,
        "Wanda, hush! You're scaring the bass!"
and so she'll tell her husband, who will say,
        "Uh-huh! Any more of these potatoes?"
and also everyone at her fortieth class reunion
        and her grandchildren and their children, too,

and they'll ignore her as well, the little ones
thinking, Whoa, G-momma's telling those old stories again!
    And on her last day, Pastor Blair will be there
saying, "That's all right, now, Wanda, you just let go,
        you hear?" And she'll wheeze and say,
"And then this fellow says, 'I can have zuh elephant
        of zuh sea'—ah, glory!"

    Up to this point in his life, Pastor Blair
will have had about him the same "divine stupidity"
        that Tennyson attributed to Garibaldi,
but the phrase "zuh elephant of zuh sea" will wake him
        right up, it'll hit him like a triple espresso,
and he'll always remember it, though he'll change
        the details as he works them into a story of his own

        about this dying member of his congregation
who raved about this particular foreign individual who,
        etc., and so forth and so on in endless retellings
which are in turn picked up by others who incorporate them
        into *their* stories until finally "zuh elephant
of zuh sea"—well, it won't be like France at all, will it,
        it'll be like Deutschland, i.e., über alles.

    And the baker, she'll say to her husband,
"Funniest thing: today this stuttering spastic hillbilly
        zombie hayseed-type dude calls me 'Sylvia Plath,'"
and her husband says, "You mean S'il Vous Plaît,
        the author of *Ariel* (1965) and *The Colossus* (1967)?"
and she'll pop herself on the forehead with a floury hand
        and say, "You know the *dates*?"

Borges at the Northside Rotary

If in the following pages there is some successful verse or other,
may the reader forgive me the audacity of having written it before him.
　　　—JORGE LUIS BORGES, *foreword to his first book of poems*

After they go to the podium and turn in their Happy Bucks
　　　and recite the Pledge of Allegiance
and the Four Truths ("Is it the Truth?
　　　　　　Is it fair to all concerned? Will it build goodwill
and better friendships? Will it be beneficial
　　　to all concerned?"), I get up to read my poetry,

and when I'm finished, one Rotarian expresses
　　　understandable confusion at exactly what it is
I'm doing and wants to know what poetry is, exactly,
　　　so I tell him that when most nonpoets think
of the word "poetry," they think of "lyric poetry,"
　　　not "narrative poetry," whereas what I'm doing

is "narrative poetry" of the kind performed
　　　by, not that I am in any way comparing myself
to them, Homer, Dante, and Milton,
　　　and he's liking this, he's smiling and nodding,
and when I finish my little speech,
　　　he shouts, "Thank you, Doctor! Thank you

for educating us!" And for the purposes
　　　of this poem, he will be known hereafter
as the Nice Rotarian. But now while I was reading,
　　　there was this other Rotarian who kept talking
all the time, just jacked his jaw right through
　　　the poet's presentations of some of the finest

vers libre available to today's listening audience,
　　　and he shall be known hereafter as the Loud Rotarian.
Nice Rotarian, Loud Rotarian: it's kind of like Good Cop,
　　　Bad Cop or God the Father, Mary the Mother.
Buy Low, Sell High. Win Some, Lose Some.
　　　Comme Ci, Comme Ça. Half Empty, Half Full.

But in a sense the Loud Rotarian was the honest one;
        he didn't like my poetry and said so—not in so many words,
but in the words he used to his tablemates
            as he spoke of his golf game or theirs
or the weather or the market or, most likely,
        some good deed that he was the spearchucker on,

the poobah, the mucky-muck, the head honcho,
        for one thing I learned very quickly
was that Rotarians are absolutely nuts
            over good deeds and send doctors to Africa
and take handicapped kids on fishing trips
        and just generally either do all sorts of hands-on

projects themselves or else raise a ton of money
        so they can get somebody else to do it for them,
whereas virtually every poet I know, myself included,
            spends his time either trying to get a line right
or else feeling sorry for himself and maybe writing a check
        once a year to the United Way if the United Way's lucky.

The Nice Rotarian was probably just agreeing with me,
        just swapping the geese and fish of his words
with the bright mirrors and pretty beads of mine,
            for how queer it is to be understood by someone
on the subject of anything, given that,
        as Norman O. Brown says, the meaning of things

is not in the things themselves but between them,
        as it surely was that time those kids scared us so bad
in Paris: Barbara and I had got on the wrong train, see,
            and when it stopped, it wasn't at the station
two blocks from our apartment but one
        that was twenty miles outside of the city,

and we looked for someone to tell us how
        to get back, but the trains had pretty much stopped
for the evening, and then out of the dark
            swaggered four Tunisian teenagers,
and as three of them circled us, the fourth
        stepped up and asked the universal ice-breaker,

i.e., Q.: Do you have a cigarette?
   A.: *Non, je ne fume pas.*
Q.: You're not French, are you?
    A.: *Non, je suis américain.* Q.: From New York?
A.: *Non, Florida.* Q.: Miami?
   A.: *Non, une petite ville qui s'appelle Tallahassee*

dans le nord de . . . And here the Tunisian kid
  mimes a quarterback passing and says, *Ah,*
l'université avec la bonne équipe de futbol!
   He was a fan of FSU sports, of all things
so we talked football for a while, and then
  he told us where to go for the last train.

Change one little thing in my life or theirs
  and they or I could have been either the Loud Rotarian
or the Nice one, and so I say to Rotarians everywhere,
   please forgive me,
my brothers, for what I have done to you
  and to myself as well,

for circumstances so influence us
  that it is more an accident
than anything else that you are listening to me
   and not the other way around,
and therefore I beg your forgiveness, my friends,
  if I wrote this poem before you did.

The invention and function of frontier humor had less to do with genial amusement than with building a psychological structure against chaos. The rattlesnake wilderness that stretched outward from Boston and Philadelphia and New York was not ready yet for drawing-room aphorisms or comedies of manners. Here lay vastness, loneliness, alienation, depravity, and many interesting varieties of sudden death.

—Ron Powers, *Dangerous Waters: A Biography of the Boy Who Became Mark Twain*

We walked to Ho Wah Garden and the Ostoneria and over to Becky's for deep-dish pizza;

to Manny's for waffles on mornings of aluminum rain;

the German butcher for bratwurst, the Greek bakery for elephant ears, the 7-11 for cocktail onions to satisfy Elizabeth's idiosyncratic cravings.

We walked until our fears resurfaced and then we ate our fears.

—CAMPBELL MCGRATH, "Spring Comes to Chicago"

The Ha-Ha, Part II: I Cry My Heart, Antonio

—at Dal Pescatore, Cannetto sull'Oglio, just outside Mantova

It's just as the waiter has brought us
      a single buttery dumpling
    stuffed with pecorino, parmigiano, and ricotta

that arrives *after* the porcini mushrooms
      and the seafood risotto
    and *before* the snapper with tomato and black olives

and the duck in balsamic vinegar reduction
      that I touch my napkin
    to my lips and say, "There are no words to describe this"

and then feel the sting of tears as I remember
      where I'd read these words,
    in that book about the trial of the English pedophile

and child murderer who delighted in recording
      the final moments
    of her victims' lives, the screaming, the promises not to tell,

her own tapes used in evidence against her yet thought so horrific
      by the judge that
    he ordered them played in a sealed courtroom

and then, in the public interest,
      to a single journalist
    who would only say, "There are no words to describe this."

And even though the waiter arrives at that moment
      to clear away plates and pour more wine
    and ask if everything is good, if it's all to our satisfaction,

still, Barbara bends close to me and asks if everything's okay,
      says I seem a little upset,
    and I cover by telling her the story that Mark's cousin Antonio

had told me about this prosciutto he'd bought
                and had put in his basement
        for curing so it would turn salty and sweet and delicate all at once,

but something went wrong, and one day
                he went down to check
        on his prosciutto, and it was maggot-ridden and moldy,

and here Antonio shakes his head and looks at me
                with a sad smile and says,
        "I cry my heart, David," and only later do I realize

I've used this story as a ha-ha, which is not a joke but a landscape trick
                from 18th-century England,
        a sunken fence used to keep cows at a picturesque distance

from the manor house so they can be seen grazing on the greensward,
                kept by the ha-ha
        from trampling the lawn and mooing at the guests.

Your ha-ha, then, is a structure against your chaos.
                And your story about Antonio's prosciutto
        is thus a structure against your psychological chaos, as the poem

about the meal at Dal Pescatore and the hideously inappropriate memory
                and Antonio's prosciutto and the ha-ha
        is a further structure against further chaos still.

Or not structure, maybe, but process, like a walk.
                There's almost no problem a walk can't solve,
        say the walkers, and surely the same is true about poetry and possibly

doubly true when the poem is about walking, as is Campbell McGrath's
                "Spring Comes to Chicago," in which
        the poet talks about walking around that city with his pregnant wife,

eating pizza in one restaurant and waffles in another and somehow surviving
                the Chicago traffic that many do *not* survive,
        for the same walk that can be our best friend can be our worst enemy as well—

while it is indisputably good to go out walking, it is equally indisputable
　　　　　that we may, in the course of our exercise,
　　　be struck down or otherwise injured, be we in 20th-century Chicago

or 18th-century Durham, where the ha-ha boom waxed and then waned
　　　　　after Lord Lambton tumbled into his,
　　　climbed out cursing, and had it filled with coal-spoil.

When the meal is over, we take a taxi to Piadena and the train
　　　　　from there to Mantova,
　　　past these little towns, each with its own *duomo,* great or small,

that bursts from the pavement like Dante's Mount of Paradise,
　　　　　and while none is so beautiful as the dome
　　　of Santa Maria del Fiore in Florence or so Gothic and spire-studded

as the Milan *duomo* that seems to be armed against the devil's legions
　　　　　or as vast as that of St. Peter's in Rome,
　　　the cathedral big enough to brag of its bigness by outlining

on its floor—plenty of opportunities to stumble there!—the plans
　　　　　of the other, lesser cathedrals,
　　　still, were we to get off the train and walk into one of these little churches,

we'd see it's been built like all the others, its interior looming larger
　　　　　than its exterior suggests and its vault
　　　painted in the manner of the night sky, because night

is the best time to talk to God, for if Satan and his boys are everywhere,
　　　　　the rates are cheaper then,
　　　and so we make our way down the aisle, the dark cut only

by candlelight, and figures shuffle in the shadows, though who they are,
　　　　　we'll never know, and our steps are uncertain,
　　　but over our heads, the sky blazes with promise, and the stars are spinning.

DATE DUE

GAYLORD   PRINTED IN U.S.A.